Ideal Business Practices

By Mitta Xinindlu

Business analysis is often overlooked by investors. Some of them forfeit many profitable opportunities due to lack of insight, and they lose lots of money. This mistake doesn't have to be the case anymore, and this book explains why.

⍰

The Market System

Financial markets offer contingencies, diversification of risks, and market specialisation to investors. On top of that, they provide an opportunity to investors to accumulate financial resources, resulting in a positive causal relationship with the economic growth. Currently, the financial markets are not stable in the United States due to a slow growth in investment and production. Investments yield returns; however, without the exclusion of risk. Due to this, investors are usually advised to allocate assets across all the major asset groups, which include commodities, currencies and securities. This strategical goal ensures a balance between risk and potential return on investment.

Considering the above, it is not advisable for investors to purchase low priced shares. The shares offered through such deals are Penny stock; for example, a share can sell below $5 in the United States, and only to discover that their actual value is below the face value. And they may be subject to change in the long run. Consider other things that are at play, such as the Initial Public Offering (IPO) which is subject to a complete process that includes an extensive market analysis and provides strategies that limit the risks to a minimum. Another aspect is that the possible rewards are high, such as of those who invested in Google in the year 2004.

Sometimes investors could be advised to purchase the shares but with caution. Despite the good records of the company, an investor purchases more risk from an IPO bearing company as compared to other stock transactions. This is because the company doesn't have a public trading experience; consequently, there is no assurance to the investors to indicate absolute returns on their investment.

Investors could consider already established companies even though the shares are of a small percentage. For instance, someone who considered investing in Coca-Cola today would not reap huge dividends. Regardless, Coca-Cola will always be a good company with which to associate. Coca-Cola's strengths include its brand equity, market share, marketing strategies, customer loyalty and company valuation. In 2016, it was ranked number three on the annual Best Global Brands, valuing its brand at an estimated amount of $73.1 billion. Considerably, Coca-Cola owns most of the market shares in the soda industry and has been leading the competition for decades. The company's 2016 revenue reports at $43.49 billion which is three times Pepsi's $11.8 billion 2016 revenue as reported by Forbes.

Using its 'happiness' marketing strategy, they maintain customer's loyalty on a consistent basis; showing this by winning an AME Gold Medallion award in 2012 and reporting a total valuation of $192.8 billion in 2016. The company's strengths can be maximized by considering its opportunities, which include logistical distribution and diversification.

Diversification includes packaging water and establishing new trade products, such as light meals. However, it has not retained a unique niche, and this is one of its weaknesses even though it has started to take part in the water trade. Other factors that can possibly weaken the continuation of Coca-Cola include the lack of health-conscious products. Such weakness hurt the brand since the world is changing in favour of the millennials who have shown to be concerned with health and diet issues. Despite its 'Coca-Cola Zero' product launch that aimed at gaining diet conscious millennials, it has not been successful. Forbes reports that there is a constant year-to-year 7% drop in Coca-Cola diet product revenues, which indicates that Coca-Cola's diet product strategy needs to be revamped.

Coca-Cola's threats include its indirect competition and water supply shortage. The shortage of water supply imposes a threat to the production of Coca-Cola liquid products. Likewise, companies such as Star Bucks and Red Bull impose a limited but consistent threat to the company's consumer segment from a competition perspective.

On a similar scale, McDonald's also remains an investors' haven. McDonald's is the world's largest fast-food chain with approximately 30,000 Franchises in 121 countries. The brand has become a symbol of globalization and the predominance of American food culture. Tantamount to the Burger King franchise, McDonald's has gained a static segment through its marketing strategies and has maintained its market share. Market analysts argue that a social presence is the core sales driver in many organizations in the current social media period. As expected,

4

McDonald's is currently visible on social media, assuring investors of its power in the fast food industry. Although the Headquarters does not have an official Snapchat account, some franchises do.

In April 2017, the Australia office offered employment opportunities through its Snapchat account. Its goal was to attract the millennials; this strategy resulted in a huge brand winning success. Today, McDonald's leads in the product market strategic influence; hits on its website are ranked at the position 1 983 in the United States and 8 218 globally, in comparison to Burger King that is graded 19 633 701 as Alexa reported in 2017. Also, between March and April 2017, the McDonald's website had been visited approximately 8 000 times, which was the lowest number in comparison to the 2016 statistics of over 10 000 hits.

Another interesting and growing hub for investors is Facebook. Facebook is by far the most relevant social platform for customer engagement due to the high number of followers who comprise of various targets. For that reason, huge companies such as McDonald's and Coca-Cola also maintain its presence on the platform even though the influence of Facebook cannot be directly measured in currency. Nonetheless, there are other ways to track and measure growth, the association to the pages of these companies indicated that the return on investment increased four times in 2012.

Reasonably, since Twitter is still a growing website, it is recommended that companies should maintain their marketing and social contact. Twitter is inclusive of the desired class with over 2.5 million users from the higher class. Another recommendation is definitely the Snapchat venture because chances of success have been proven to be higher than the Instagram platform. In consideration of the statistics as per the reports, Burger King is dominant, even though its following is low in traditional markets. Its consumers are passionate about the products.

Considerably, companies should increase their market share by transposing their images from Instagram and post them as blog posts. This could entice the need for its products and incite passion and pride. It could also increase social media reach in terms of discussion, retweets, reposts, and post sharing. It's true and unavoidable, existing consumers are in demand for excessive social consumption.

Integrity in Business

The main traits of ethical behaviour such as these three have been prompted in various fields of trade. For example, in 1983, Crawford emphasized their significance in establishing methodical processes in the administration of higher education. Similarly, event management, as a professional trade, requires the same traits for organizations to run effectively. The concept of integrity is accepted as a reference that guides the choices of humanity. It presumes a notion of honesty. The idea of integrity represents the motive as objectivity and honesty. Integrity as a behavioural trait is defined as the ability of a person to rely on one's principles despite other people's opinions.

Leaders, such as event managers, are expected to commit to conduct in a manner that advocates the public's expectations. This definition suggests that the opinion of the public is relevant to measuring the trust and support that is essential to managers. Event managers play prominent roles in an organization and their contributions are measurable in profit margins. For example, for every expense spent in an event, the income is retained through sponsorships, donations, and contract alliances. The scope of their work places them at the forefront of the business and their actions can be studied by both internal and external participants. Thus, any behavioural conduct is a representation of the company. Should an event manager behave in an unethical manner, the implications can be detrimental to the status of the business.

It is reported that a volunteer at a social event broke his spinal cord due to negligence by the event manager of the annual World Champion Punkin Chunkin festival. The volunteer's name is Daniel Fair; according to his statement, he fell off an all-terrain vehicle which also pressed on his body. Instead of suing the owners of the vehicle, it is argued that the action was legally correct. In his stance, he reiterated the responsibilities of event organizers in ensuring safety for those who are in attendance at the event. Anyway, in dispute, the event manager argued that Fair had signed a waiver which allocated all risk and responsibilities upon himself.

In 2009, McDonald's Corporation lost $ 6.1 million resulting in the failure of managing events effectively. The actions were viewed as threatening to the society of Kentucky, USA, resulting in consumers contemplating the standards of the food chain provider. When corporate actions threaten to destruct the public, their business licenses can be repealed, fines and other penalties may be imposed under the law, or citizens may withdraw patronage and profits, thereby risking the continuity of the business. As it is evident from this case, the event manager's lack of action against unethical behaviour damages the brand and results in financial loss.

Of course, it must be noted that although a customer may sign a waiver, the responsibility of the event manager does not shift. Thus, the manager must still uphold the duties as defined in the job specification without attempting to pass blame. Clients are the epitome of any business, and if one client is not satisfied, it should be an indicative factor that improvements should be made. The task of an event manager is also ensuring that those who form part of the brand, can feel proud to be associated with it.

The 21st century introduced transparency in terms of the actions of businesses and their representatives. Social media, Twitter, for example, is a platform that event managers use on a regular basis to maintain the visibility of their organizations. Also, this is where they often communicate with their potential customers. Hence, the tacit and implicit actions of event managers are considered under the measures of moral and ethical principles as the norm. In 2013, Epicurious, a digital brand in service to customers in the cooking industry, misrepresented their organization as insensitive. Their market strategy misused the tragedy of the Boston bombing that took place in America to promote sales. Nevertheless, this action enraged Twitter users, as a result, they sent confrontational tweets which were directed at the brand. Although there is no actual loss of business that is reported in numbers, the company later apologized. Socially, their reputation was already refuted and described as unethical and immoral by news outlets.

In a similar case, although bearing different merits, event managers of the FIFA world cup acted unethically in the representation of their organizations. They are reported to be a part of a ten-year fraud syndicate, which resulted in certain countries receiving the opportunity to hold the event; an amount of $150 million fraud, money laundering, and bribery was exchanged. This case reflects mistrust and immoral behaviour; in addition, it highlights their lack of integrity.

In this case, the indictment, among countries, also included Traffic Sports International and Traffic Sports USA which are profit-focused corporates. Due to their behaviour, the discussed event managers are in jail, while others are on trial. It is evident that unethical behaviour has negative implications. These implications could be in the form of financial loss, reputational damage, mistrust in the organization, and lack of confidence in the events managers. It is advised that managers must uphold their leadership roles and represent companies ethically, especially when an event manager's role is to maintain business relationships. In fact, managers are the brand ambassadors of their companies and any of their action is a direct reflection of their organization. Integrity, objectivity and honesty indicate firm leadership, regardless of culture, the form of business, or clientele; and an ethical behaviour can protect businesses from the negative implications of the opposite.

Building Profitable Investments

There are many dreamers who change their reams into big investments. Take Walt Disney, for an example. Walt Disney' life was driven by four Cs; he once confirmed in an interview that curiosity, confidence, constancy and courage were the basis of his success. Born in Illinois, the United States in 1901 where his career commenced twenty years later. Subsequently, starting a studio that has now become the best cartoon company in the world. In the admiration of his success, this article aims to explore the prominent moments that defined his niche in the animation field.

Similarly to many entrepreneurial stories, the act of being fired from his first job motivated Walt to establish his enterprise despite his lack of successes initially due to a small consumer segment. His second business venture afforded him enough resources to expand and recruit more animators who could assist in expanding Laugh-O-Grams, a company that he started with his partner, Fred Herman. According to the government archives, one can observe that Laugh-O-Grams had a start-up capital of $15000; nevertheless, this initiative ended in bankruptcy. Disney's strategy was to modernize classic tales; accordingly, not only did this create a need for his talent, it also promoted the importance of animation.

Rudy Ising, who is the found of Warner Brothers and MGM cartoon network, mentored Walt, providing the necessary skills and business acumen. After several additional attempts, in 1928 Disney managed to draw the first anime of what would be popular for a century: Mickey Mouse. The success was not immediate, but he managed to grow the company and began to make its brand known. With the beginning of the feature films, Walt took on a new strategy between 1937 and 1954. Today, the international success of the Disney studios is prominent and there have not been any immediate competitors who have had a similar influence.

By the end of the 1940s, after the Disneyland theme park was established, Walt had further developed his goals. The park was modelled with entertainment attractions which enabled customers to view the impressions of his characters in real life. As it was a norm at the time to reject new and modernized initiatives, people were hesitant to consider his project. Even though Disney studios had already proved itself in the cinemas, only a few trusted Walt for his proposed new project. Another hindering factor was that the project had a cost that required him to raise funds, which he did not have at the time. Although he had consulted with several banks to secure a loan, his request was unsuccessful.

It took him a rejection from 302 banks before he finally secured a financial agreement. Consequently, the Disney Empire expanded in 1955. In this regard, Walt's life story reflects how one can change failures and into success. He had a remarkable imagination, drive, and humour. He was a visionary and a dreamer. He believed that humans could achieve whatever they aspired.

In his profession, he prioritized hard work, individualism, and optimism. He similarly showed this in his classic marketing tactics which required that a customer's wants and needs be considered before production commenced. It can be concluded that his vision was based on making people happy. Moreover, he did not cater to only children but to all age groups. Walt created opportunities even though many circumstances indicated that he would fail.

In conclusion, Walt Disney's influence is enormous. In affirmation, he has been awarded many prizes for different genres in his career, including the Academy Honorary Award that he obtained in 1932, 1939, and 1942. This comic strip entrepreneur turned his wind into a breeze of accolades. His belief in the 4 Cs is now an example for the younger generation to persevere and never give up.

He studied the market and realised what he needed to offer. In business, a market research is an economic and social structure that transfers product knowledge between consumers and companies. To exist in a competitive environment, the company must satisfy its customers while generating a profit. Thus, to satisfy customers, the company must be knowledgeable of the customers' needs. Therefore, knowing their needs requires extensive research.

In this context, market research can influence decision-making in instances of introducing new products, restructuring old processes, entering a new market segment, and adopting new trends. An organization can consider new technological changes and seek ways that the changes can be used to the advantage of the business. Often, this can be utilized to win a competitive advantage against direct and indirect competitors.

Samsung is at the forefront in confirming the necessity for an effective research strategy. In external diagnosis, for example, Samsung excludes the bulk specialization at the level of demand. Samsung in its customer research considers the competition, and this was demonstrated when Samsung allegedly stole a software design from Apple, in which case it was found guilty. Apple alleged that its patent design and colour coordination had been copied by Samsung.

Nonetheless, although the decision was unethical, Samsung demonstrates to have the sense to complete a thorough market research to identify the best product that has a potential to increase sales and attain customer loyalty. Apart from the competition factor, their decision, as reports state, is influenced by the research results. In the research, it analyses the influence of several factors, the main ones being: age, size, strategy, technology, and the impact of the external environment.

If an investor, an entrepreneur or a simple market analyst wants to dive deeper into market research, they must consider all relevant factors, such as sampling methods, population, and methods. A sampling procedure is used to obtain an estimate of certain factors of the research population in which the sampling system is judged by the quality of the estimates obtained. In some cases, distinct estimates may be like the true value or may differ and give a poor measure of the merits of the system. The best sampling method, in this regard, gives a remote estimate of the true value whereas an average one gives an estimate very close to the true value. Also, a procedure is best judged by the frequency distribution of the many estimates that could be obtained by a repeated sampling. It is also paramount when it gives a frequency distribution with a small variance and an estimate of the mean very close to the true value.

In sampling, there can be irregularities. One of the common irregularities is the difference between an estimate of the mean and the true value which is called bias. It is also used to designate the process by which this difference occurs. In emphasis, the amplitude of the bias and that of the variance of a sampling system are significantly independent. For example, a procedure can give an estimate with both a small variance and a large deviation; consequently, causing all the estimates to differ from the true value. Another example is that in marketing research a table of measures with nearly unreadable figures on the scale would present some additional variance, and a table with the scale moved on one side would introduce a bias.

When conducting a consumer needs-based study, bias is frequently triggered by a poor analytical technique, but more often it originates from insufficient sample selection or from a poor method used to calculate the measurements or to attain them. For instance, in cases where one must increase the sample size or combine the data from two or more samples, the bias can remain unaffected. In converse, the variance is reduced. Bias decreases the level of validity in research. Thus, for the best results, the best sampling procedure should be free of it. In addition, to achieve the required level of precision, it is recommended that appropriate samples should be considered.

Ultimately, the goal of the best sample is to obtain a given level of accuracy and with the least cost. To accomplish this, one must set the appropriate research questions which will be used to obtain information from the selected participants. Additionally, the correct scale should be selected accordingly. The reason for this is that when a specified level of accuracy has been achieved in the sampling procedure, additional developments cannot influence the result.

Similarly and depending on the goal and the availability of resources, one must use the correct method; for example, probability sampling is more appropriate in many cases, such as stratified random sampling if one wishes to have many but small samples; quota method where one has an already defined number of participants; selective method where one's research determines which target to use; and convenience method if the targeted sample is known or close to the research environment. Probability sampling is also preferable because it offers an equal chance for everyone to be selected in the sample. By providing an opportunity to all, it means that bias is also reduced.

To obtain the best sampling procedure, one must collect the required and necessary information about the targeted population, sample it either using the probability method or the

non-probability one to standardize the results of the research.

Technology Affects the Product Adoption Stage

A digital divide is the disparity of access to computer technologies and especially the Internet. It is not only about infrastructure and connectivity issues, but more generally about access to content and knowledge. Today, half the world's population uses the internet, accounting for 50 percent which is 3.2 billion people as reported in 2015.

In 2016, for example, approximately 10 percent of Canadians did not have access to the internet. Although digital inequalities have lessened on a global scale, there are those who are still deprived of access to the internet and who are marginalized from the main societal trends. These people include elderly persons, non-graduates, and rural individuals. Due to their exclusion from the digital sphere, they become victims of the inequality in content distribution. This essay explores the meaning of a digital divide and in relation to participatory culture in a world of Web 2.0.

People who do not use the Internet now belong to groups of the population: 83 percent of them are over 60 years of age, 90 percent of whom do not any form of access, and 33 percent have incomes of less than 1000 Dollar per month. The digital divide can be categorised to define the affected groups. These groups are based on different but similar forms of the digital divide which are generational, geographical, social, professional, voluntary, and classification divide.

The internet has created a new generation of individuals whose lives are mostly depended on it. Some members of this generation have also established companies that operate digitally, such as Online-government, Online-commerce, digital educational institutions, and social media. Evidently, these are not without disadvantages. Digital usage of this generation can be excessive, addictive, and cyber abusive. But most dangerously, it can disclose their confidential information and expose them to other forms of cybercrime. The older generation who grew up in a world deprived of technology is reluctant to merge with the digital generation due to these reasons. Progressively, the generational gap decreases as the older generation dies and the younger generation grows older.

Geographical inequality of access to networks is mostly visible in rural and high mountain areas where connectivity is a challenge. In Canada, a high margin in the rural areas is not digitally connected as compared to the majority of those who live in the city. Only a few individuals have access to 4G, the rest operate from 2G and 3G, as reported. Similarly, the social divide separates users from non-users based on their income, profession, different modes of connection, and the access and affordability to advanced digital equipment. Those who feel that they must maintain a high social standard usually adapt themselves to maintain their social class.

The differences in their profession also create a digital divide since only 90 percent of those who work in offices have full access to the internet. Those who do not have access become a minority that is a target to cultural and commercial marginalization. On the contrary, there are those who exclude themselves voluntarily. These individuals have the opportunity and means to have a digital connection, however, due to finding no value in it, they choose to be isolated. Their reasons range from lack of stimuli to time wastage. Correspondingly, the last group is based on class: cultural background, beliefs, and isolation. These individuals are excluded because of their religion; they are isolated in the form of direct imprisonment or other forms of incarceration.

The digital gap impact can be minimized by redefining consumers as also producers and suppliers of content. In this manner, people will collaborate and increase their social capabilities. This is based on the claim that participatory culture is a society that has minimal obstructions to creativity and social discussions, which has a solid support structure for innovative ideas, in which mentorship opportunities are availed, and where participants are connected to one another and value each other's opinions.

The participatory culture affords individuals an opportunity to obtain competencies and skills that are necessary for social connectivity. Such competencies include multitasking, objectivity, communication, simulation, and collective intelligence. As a result, this culture becomes a transformation from an authoritative organisation to a platform in which media takes a

26

democratic stance. In emphasis, the new media, as it is known, break the barriers that are formed on aesthetic, political, economic, and cognitive methodologies.

The abundance or lack of resources constitutes in which side in the digital divide induvial fall. Those who have less are constantly excluded from participating in the internet culture, thus, creating an exclusive cultural society whose participation is predetermined according to their resources. The noted barriers are culturally converged by dislocating resistance and isolation. Arguably, schools and parents have can influence the roles of their children by teaching them about collaboration, doing so enables their participation from as early as required. Any form of a development, association, or learning is prominent a factor in a participatory culture. In addition, with such factors, the Web 2.0 society will be collaborative.

Relevance of Adverts

An advertising campaign is a marketing communication of products or services. Its target can be towards the actual sale of goods, creation of brand awareness, the acquisition of internet users through online shopping, and the retention of existing and loyal clients through subscriptions. The presence of companies on social networks has become an essential component of marketing and advertising strategies. Depending on the needs and budgets of companies, a strategy can include advertisements on platforms such as Facebook. The approach is also made possible by the sponsored solutions proposed by such platforms. In specificity, the advertising campaign that is concerned was placed on Facebook, Instagram, Twitter, and YouTube.

Companies' business orientation is based on advertising to a segment of millions and millions of consumers daily. The growth of following is also high and very rapid. For example, a company with 45,000 Facebook followers, 200,000 Twitter followers, 60,000 Instagram followers, and over 500,000 subscriptions on YouTube is enough to cut down advertising expenses by almost

80%. Also, due to word-of-mouth advertising, the strength of the campaign is usually multiplied two times the number of the social 'following'. To achieve this, the marketing team needs to create an effective advertising strategy that could communicate the benefits of the item in a cost-effective method. Such a strategy distinguished a new product from its existing merchandise and from those of its competitors. It achieves this by highlighting specific qualities and communicating the way the product would be efficient in consumers' lifestyles. Targeting the mass audience by making use of social network database is based on interest, media usage, and demographics.

Businesses today must communicate the appropriate message to the suitable consumers; thus, proving that it understands their needs. Advertising will remain part of the business whether done through social media or the traditional way.

The Survival of Oligopolies

An oligopoly market is a place where a small number of producers control the economy. These companies are often characterized by their strategic interaction and interdependence of behaviours. Each enterprise is aware that its actions will influence the choices of their competitors. Because of this, it forms a strategy in consideration of the competition and has a non-negligible influence on the market price. This type of a market is vastly concentrated.

Due to these characteristics, a new company must align its strategy with the interdependent nature of the market. However, it must also consider its approach by clearly identifying a niche which it can retain successfully, and this can be economical when the product or services being offered are unique. The entry target market can be localized in a different geographical area where the influence of already existing competitors is minimal. Some companies' best option is a strategic alliance with the big other companies due to limitations in the offer of alternative and affordability. Be implementing such a brilliant collaboration, organisations earn a great access to an already existing share even though it is at a cost.

There are three recommendable entry strategies in such a market: strategic partnerships, majority share acquisition, and Greenfield investment. Oligopoly companies are determined by concentration ratios; these determine the fractions of the market share; thus, making it difficult for new companies to obtain a sustainable share. Patenting is commendable because it grants a protection against possible duplication of the product. In the long run, a patent makes it possible to obtain an absolute control over an invention. Partnering with them allows him to quickly learn how to beat the competition without aggravating it to the negative level.

The factors that differentiate many entrepreneurs include their entry strategies. Some hope to compete and win against the already existing firms without depending on them. Unfortunately, they oversee to consider a critical defining trait of the market. Secondly, they become stubborn and ignore necessary partnership. By contrast, for example, Bill Gates patented his software and built a partnership with the already existing company that had most of the market share. This enabled him to build relationships with stakeholders which made it easy for him to capture the market.

After over a half-century later, another visionary car maker, Elon Musk emerges with an electric car of Tesla. Tesla, a company formed by a South African born, and has had many failures in the early stages of its market entry which resulted from several factors such as product failure and disbelief in the product. Tesla is not an automaker that has differentiated itself from other manufacturing by focusing on the demand for electric cars. This niche was small at the beginning; however, it has grown over the years and big companies such as BMW are considering producing similar products.

Tesla has sold approximately 80,000 vehicles since 2012, 50% of it in 2014. The plant currently produces more than 1,000 units a week. It identified itself with a concentration of intellectual capital, with which it has managed to capture its consumers and those of the competitors. Currently, it has partnered with Daimler AG and Panasonic, which indicate its continued growth and recognition in the market.

Investors and businesses owners should also be wise in their dealings by considering all the aspects of business with seriousness and rigour.

www.ingramcontent.com/pod-product-compliance
Lightning Source LLC
Chambersburg PA
CBHW021851170526
45157CB00006B/2397